SRI HARMANDIR SAHIB

Simon Rose

MEDIA ENHANCED BOOKS

AV2 BY WEIGL

ADDED VALUE • AUDIO VISUAL

www.av2books.com

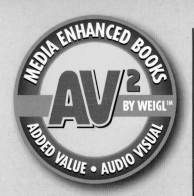

AV² provides enriched content that supplements and complements this book. Weigl's AV² books strive to create inspired learning and engage young minds in a total learning experience.

Your AV² Media Enhanced books come alive with...

Audio
Listen to sections of the book read aloud.

Video
Watch informative video clips.

Embedded Weblinks
Gain additional information for research.

Try This!
Complete activities and hands-on experiments.

Key Words
Study vocabulary, and complete a matching word activity.

Quizzes
Test your knowledge.

Slide Show
View images and captions, and prepare a presentation.

... and much, much more!

Go to **www.av2books.com**, and enter this book's unique code.

BOOK CODE

L889963

AV² by Weigl brings you media enhanced books that support active learning.

Published by AV² by Weigl
350 5th Avenue, 59th Floor
New York, NY 10118
Websites: www.av2books.com   www.weigl.com

Library of Congress Cataloging-in-Publication Data
Rose, Simon, 1961-
 Sri Harmandir Sahib / Simon Rose.
    pages cm. -- (Houses of faith)
Includes index.
 ISBN 978-1-4896-2609-7 (hardcover : alk. paper) -- ISBN 978-1-4896-2613-4 (softcover : alk. paper) -- ISBN 978-1-4896-2617-2 (single-user ebook) --
ISBN 978-1-4896-2621-9 (multi-user ebook)
1. Golden Temple (Amritsar, India)--Juvenile literature. 2. Sikh temples--India--Amritsar--Juvenile literature. 3. Amritsar (India)--Buildings, structures, etc.--Juvenile literature. I. Title.
 BL2018.36.A472G6474 2014
 294.6'350954552--dc23
                    2014036719

Printed in the United States of America in North Mankato, Minnesota
1 2 3 4 5 6 7 8 9 0 18 17 16 15 14

112014
WEP311214

Editor: Heather Kissock
Design: Mandy Christiansen

Every reasonable effort has been made to trace ownership and to obtain permission to reprint copyright material. The publishers would be pleased to have any errors or omissions brought to their attention so that they may be corrected in subsequent printings. Weigl acknowledges Getty Images, Alamy, Corbis, iStockphoto, and Dreamstime as its primary image suppliers for this title.

Contents

What Is the Sri Harmandir Sahib?

The Sri Harmandir Sahib glitters in the sunlight of Amritsar, India. Known as the holiest **shrine** in the Sikh religion, the building is often called the Golden Temple because of its gold-covered exterior. Sikhs from all over the world come to Amritsar to worship at the shrine. Over the years, the building has also become a popular tourist destination.

Constructed between 1588 and 1601, the Sri Harmandir Sahib is one of the oldest places of worship for Sikhs. It is the central part of a larger complex that includes a clock tower, an assembly hall, and a large dining area. The shrine itself is surrounded by a large pool of water called a sarovar. People often bathe in the waters of the sarovar, which are believed to have healing properties.

The shrine represents the distinct identity and heritage of the Sikhs. However, it also extends a broader reach, standing as a symbol of equality and brotherhood. For this reason, people of all faiths are welcome to visit and worship at the Sri Harmandir Sahib.

A Sikh house of worship is called a gurdwara. This means "the gateway to the guru."

The Sikh Faith

The Sikh faith, or Sikhism, began in the 15th century in northern India. It is based on the teachings of Nanak, the religion's first **guru**. Sikhs believe in one god called Waheguru. Guru Nanak taught that Waheguru could be understood through **meditation**. Sikhs are committed to working hard, living honestly, sharing with others, and giving to those less fortunate. To show their devotion to their religion, Sikhs wear symbols of faith called the Five Ks. Kesh, or uncut hair, symbolizes holiness and strength. The kangha is a small comb that is kept tucked in the hair. It represents a clean body and spirit. A steel bracelet called a kara is worn to remind Sikhs that they are connected to a larger community. The kirpan is a short dagger carried by Sikhs at all times. It represents the defense of the good and the weak. The kachera are long undershorts. They stand for self-control.

Sikhism is one of the world's **youngest** religions.

10

gurus shaped the Sikh religion over 300 years.

More than
21 million

Sikhs live in India. At least 75 percent of these Sikhs live in the state of Punjab.

Sikhism is the 5th largest religion in the world.

- Christianity 2.2 billion
- Islam 1.6 billion
- Hinduism 1 billion
- Buddhism 500 million
- Sikhism 30 million

A Step Back in Time

The building of the Sri Harmandir Sahib rose out of a larger plan to establish a community in northwest India. Construction of this community started in 1570 and included the **excavation** of land to create a sarovar. The sarovar was completed in 1577. By this time, the town of Amritsar had formed around it.

Guru Arjan Dev, the fifth Sikh guru, saw the need for a place of worship in the town. He decided to build a shrine where Sikhs could gather to pray and worship. The construction process took about 13 years. When the building was completed, it became the home of the Guru Granth Sahib, the **holy scripture** of the Sikh faith.

CONSTRUCTION TIMELINE

1588 The **foundation stone** of the Sri Harmandir Sahib is laid.

1764 Reconstruction work is undertaken on the damaged shrine and its sarovar.

1570   **1600**   **1650**   **1700**   **1765**

1570 Construction of the sarovar begins. It is completed seven years later.

1601 Construction of the shrine is completed.

1757 to 1764 The shrine is severely damaged during war with the Afghans.

The building did not have its gold decoration when it was first erected. This was added in the 1800s as part of a **restoration** program. The Sri Harmandir Sahib had experienced years of damage due to attacks from enemy forces. It had to be almost completely rebuilt.

Today, Amritsar is the largest city in the state of Punjab. It serves as an important commercial and cultural hub for northern India.

1802 Work begins to cover the exterior of the shrine with **gold plate**.

1993 A new restoration project is launched to repair the Sri Harmandir Sahib complex.

2004 A water treatment and **filtration** plant is installed to maintain the quality of the Sri Harmandir Sahib's water.

| 1800 | 1875 | 1950 | 1975 | 2010 |

1830 The restoration work on the shrine complex is completed.

1984 The Indian Army attacks **militants** in the Sri Harmandir Sahib complex. Some of the buildings are heavily damaged.

Sri Harmandir Sahib's Location

The Sri Harmandir Sahib is located in the older part of Amritsar. It is situated on land in the center of the sarovar and is connected to the mainland by a **causeway**. The shrine's placement in the center of the sarovar represents the union of the spiritual and physical worlds.

DARSHANI DEORI The causeway has an arch at the shore end called the Darshani Deori. The arch has a frame measuring 10 feet (3 meters) high and 8.5 feet (2.6 m) wide.

CAUSEWAY The causeway leading into the shrine is 202 feet (61.6 m) long and 21 feet (6.4 m) wide.

SAROVAR The sarovar surrounding the Sri Harmandir Sahib covers an area of 150 square feet (13.9 square meters).

When first built, the Sri Harmandir Sahib was surrounded by forest. Since then, a number of buildings important to the Sikh faith have been built around it. At the end of the causeway, for instance, is the Akal Takht, the administrative center for the religion.

The building appears to be floating on the surface of the water. However, the first floor is built below the water's surface. People have to go down steps to enter the building. This is to ensure that they feel humble when entering this holy place.

Amritsar

INDIA

Bay of Bengal

Arabian Sea

N

0   400 Kilometers
0   400 Miles

MAIN BUILDING The shrine building covers an area of 40.5 square feet (3.8 sq. m).

PLATFORM The Sri Harmandir Sahib stands on a rectangular platform, which is 67 square feet (6.2 sq. m) in size.

Touring the Exterior

*The Sri Harmandir Sahib was built as a symbol of the Sikh faith. Many of its design features reflect the beliefs and culture of Sikhs. However, the architecture is a blend of Hindu and **Muslim** styles.*

WALLS The Sri Harmandir Sahib's exterior walls are the best-known features of the building. The lower walls are **clad** in white marble panels that are decorated with animal and floral designs. The upper walls are also made from marble. However, this marble has been covered with gold plating. The gold covering extends to the top of the shrine, including the towers and main dome.

DOMES The top floor of the Sri Harmandir Sahib features several domes. The largest dome sits in the center of the floor, resting over a small room. Called the Golden Dome, it is shaped like an inverted lotus flower, which points back to Earth. The lotus represents the Sikhs' concern for the problems facing the world. Each of the shrine's four towers are also capped by domes. A series of smaller domes run along the **parapet**.

PARDAKSHNA The pardakshna is the pathway that surrounds the shrine. It leads to the Har ki Pauri, which means "Steps of Almighty God." The steps are located at the rear of the building. They face the morning Sun in the east and go down into the sarovar. Visitors to the shrine can descend the steps to drink from the water.

The parikarma is a path around the outer edges of the sarovar. Sikhs walk around the path in a clockwise direction before crossing the causeway to the Sri Harmandir Sahib.

Every evening, the Guru Granth Sahib is taken from the Sri Harmandir Sahib and stored in the Akal Takht. In the morning, it is returned to the shrine in an elaborate ceremony.

The causeway is also known as the Guru's Bridge.

A flight of stairs leads visitors to the Darshani Deori. Once through the gateway, people descend toward the causeway into the shrine.

Visitors to the Sri Harmandir Sahib are welcome to visit the langar, or community kitchen, at the south end of the complex to receive a free meal.

The dome-capped parapet forms a wall around the shrine's main dome. At each corner of the wall is a tower that is topped with a dome of its own.

The pardakshna is 13 feet (4 m) **wide**.

The shrine's langar feeds at least

100,000
people every day.

220 pounds
(100 kilograms) of gold were used to cover the shrine.

The parapet that surrounds the building's roof is
4 feet
(1.2 m) high.

The roof of the first floor is
26 feet 9 inches
(8.2 m) in height.

A maharaja, or prince, donated
500,000 rupees
for the purchase of the original gold plating.

Inside the Sri Harmandir Sahib

The Sri Harmandir Sahib opens its doors to people of all backgrounds. While it remains a place of worship, visitors are welcome to walk through the shrine's rooms and view objects that are important to the Sikh faith.

ENTRANCES The Sri Harmandir Sahib has four entrances, one on each side of the building. The entrances face north, south, east, and west. The four entrances are meant to show that Sikhism has respect for and openness to people of all faiths. The doors to the shrine remain open for much of the day. People can begin entering the shrine as early as 2:00 AM. The doors usually close around 10:30 PM each day.

MAIN HALL The main hall is located on the first floor of the building. Also called the darbar, the hall is the center for religious activity in the Sri Harmandir Sahib. The walls have carved wooden panels and **inlaid** marble. There are also paintings and decorations made of silver and gold.

SHISH MAHAL This highly decorative room is located on the shrine's second floor. It is also called the Mirror Room. This is because its walls and ceilings are decorated with small pieces of mirror. The mirrors are many different sizes, shapes, and colors. Many of the designs are of flowers. People can come to the Shish Mahal to hear verses from the Guru Granth Sahib recited.

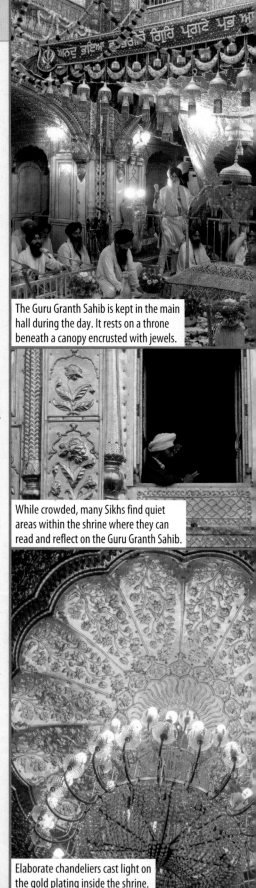

The Guru Granth Sahib is kept in the main hall during the day. It rests on a throne beneath a canopy encrusted with jewels.

While crowded, many Sikhs find quiet areas within the shrine where they can read and reflect on the Guru Granth Sahib.

Elaborate chandeliers cast light on the gold plating inside the shrine.

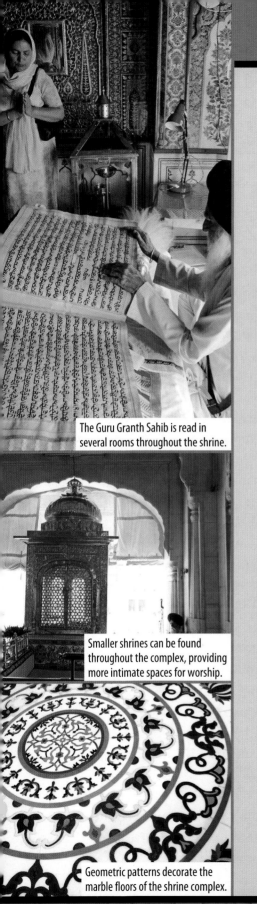

The Guru Granth Sahib is read in several rooms throughout the shrine.

Smaller shrines can be found throughout the complex, providing more intimate spaces for worship.

Geometric patterns decorate the marble floors of the shrine complex.

Sikh priests recite the Guru Granth Sahib throughout the day. Each priest reads aloud for **3 hours**.

All visitors must **remove** their shoes and **wash** their feet before entering the Sri Harmandir Sahib.

The walls of the shrine are decorated with about 300 different patterns.

After the Sri Harmandir Sahib **closes for the day,** the main hall is **washed with milk**.

Visitors may not drink alcohol, smoke, or eat meat inside the building.

The Science behind the Sri Harmandir Sahib

The building of the Sri Harmandir Sahib and its sarovar was a long and complicated project. Great care was taken during the construction of the sarovar. The builders had to think of ways to keep the water clean for bathing. They also wanted to make sure that the water would not damage the structure over time. When planning the shrine itself, the builders worked to ensure that the materials used would be long-lasting, and have the ability to showcase important symbols of the Sikh faith.

THE SAROVAR When first built, the sarovar's walls were made of the earth around it. Over time, people made changes to the sarovar to improve the quality of the water. One of the first changes was to add **masonry** walls around the sides of the structure. The material that lines the walls is said to be weed-resistant. This limits the number of organisms that can enter the water. At first, the sarovar was only filled with rainwater. Today, water is delivered to the sarovar by **aqueduct** from the Ravi River. This water contains minerals that help to protect it from germs. A new filtration system was also added to the sarovar. This system removes sand and other foreign objects from the water before it enters the sarovar.

THE PLATFORM AND CAUSEWAY The Sri Harmandir Sahib and its causeway had to be protected from the surrounding water when they were built. Over time, the movement of the water could cause damage to the structure. The **substructure** of the Sri Harmandir Sahib and causeway has a number of **vaulted** tunnels. This allows the water in the sarovar to easily flow back and forth. The structure is stronger and longer-lasting as a result.

MARBLE Marble was one of the main materials used in building the Sri Harmandir Sahib. Marble is hard-wearing and lasts a long time. However, it is also known as a soft rock. This means that it can be easily cut and shaped. The measurement of hardness scale (Mohs) determines the hardness of a stone based on how it can be scratched by hard objects. On this scale, marble measures 3 out of 10. Marble's softness allowed the **artisans** involved in building the Sri Harmandir Sahib to carve intricate designs into the shrine's floor tiles and its interior and exterior wall panels.

The vaulted tunnels that form the shrine's substructure give the building stability on the water.

Every few years, the sarovar is emptied and given a major cleaning. This cleaning is called kar seva.

Fish in the sarovar eat algae and other organisms to keep the water clean.

Most of the marble detailing in the shrine dates back to the 1800s.

Sri Harmandir Sahib's Builders

Many people were involved in building and rebuilding the Sri Harmandir Sahib. The early gurus of the Sikh faith played major roles in the construction of the building. The rulers of the area made changes in the following centuries. The Sri Harmandir Sahib and its complex has also been maintained and renovated by the local and national governments.

Guru Ram Das Guru Ram Das played a key role in laying the groundwork for the construction of the Sri Harmandir Sahib. Born in 1534, in what is now Lahore, Pakistan, he became the fourth Sikh guru in 1574. Guru Ram Das was responsible for founding the city of Amritsar. He began work on the city's sarovar, which eventually became the site of the Sri Harmandir Sahib. Besides this work, Guru Ram Das wrote many poetic verses that were later added to the Guru Granth Sahib. He also wrote other verses and hymns that are important to the daily lives of Sikhs. Guru Ram Das died in 1581. His youngest son succeeded him as guru.

Baba Budha Ji Baba Budha Ji was born in 1506. He was closely associated with the first six Sikh gurus and is one of the most revered figures in Sikhism. Baba Budha Ji supervised the excavation of the sarovar for the Sri Harmandir Sahib. The tree under which he sat during the work still exists in the shrine complex. Baba Budha Ji was the first priest, or Granthi, of the Sri Harmandir Sahib. He also laid the foundations for most of the holy buildings in Amritsar. Baba Budha Ji lived for more than 100 years. He died in 1631.

The construction of the Sri Harmandir Sahib led to a Sikh school of architecture that was unique from the Hindu and Muslim styles found throughout India at the time.

Guru Arjan Dev Guru Arjan Dev was born in 1563. He was the fifth guru of the Sikh faith. He worked with his father, Guru Ram Das, on the construction of Amritsar's sarovar and organized the construction of the Sri Harmandir Sahib. Guru Arjan Dev played a key role in the creation of several communities, including Santokhsar, Tarn Taran Sahib, and Sri Hargobindpur, and ensured that each community had a shrine and sarovar of its own. Guru Arjan Dev wrote more than 2,000 poetic verses. He also collected the songs and poems of previous gurus. These were used to create the text of the Guru Granth Sahib. In the early 17th century, the Indian government became worried about the popularity of Sikhism and took steps to lessen its presence in the country. Guru Arjan Dev was the first Sikh **martyr** to suffer for his beliefs. He died in 1606, after being tortured.

Ranjit Singh Ranjit Singh was born in 1780. He was the founder and maharaja of the Sikh kingdom of the Punjab in northern India. He became the maharaja in 1801 at the age of 20. Ranjit Singh fought many battles as he expanded his empire in the early 19th century. He was known as Sher-e-Punjab, or the Lion of Punjab. Ranjit Singh ordered much of the marble and gold decoration at the Sri Harmandir Sahib. He also built two important Sikh shrines in memory of the 10th Sikh guru, Guru Gobind Singh. Takht Sri Patna Sahib was built at the guru's birthplace, while Takht Sachkhand Sri Hazur Sahib was erected in the city of Nanded. Ranjit Singh also renovated other sacred Sikh sites during his reign. He died in 1839.

Similar Structures around the World

The Sri Harmandir Sahib is one of the world's best-known gurdwaras. However, there are other gurdwaras that hold special significance to Sikhs. Key decisions about the religious and social life of the Sikh community have been made in some of these gurdwaras. Others pay tribute to the gurus that founded the Sikh religion.

Takht Sachkhand Sri Hazur Sahib

BUILT: 1837
LOCATION: Nanded, Maharashtra, India
DESIGN: Ranjit Singh
DESCRIPTION: Located along the Godavari River, Takht Sachkhand Sri Hazur Sahib is one of Five Takhts of the Sikh faith. These five buildings are a series of gurdwaras that are considered **seats** of the Sikh religion. The gurdwara was built on the site where Guru Gobind Singh died in 1708. The temple is two stories tall. Its interior follows a design similar to the Sri Harmandir Sahib. However, while the Sri Harmandir Sahib has gold plating on its exterior, Sri Hazur Sahib's gold plates are found inside, on the walls of the temple's inner room.

The entire complex containing the Takht Sachkhand Sri Hazur Sahib covers several acres (hectares) and includes two other smaller shrines.

Gurdwara Sri Tarn Taran Sahib

BUILT: 1590s
LOCATION: Tarn Taran, Punjab, India
DESIGN: Guru Arjan Dev
DESCRIPTION: Built in honor of Guru Ram Das, this gurdwara is a three-story building that sits on a platform with a marble floor. Like the Sri Harmandir Sahib, the top part of the building is covered with gold-plated sheets. The temple's dome has an ornamental gold **pinnacle** with an umbrella-shaped decoration on the top. Inside, the walls and ceiling are decorated with glass and intricate **stucco** designs. The gurdwara has one of the largest sarovars in the Sikh community.

The Gurdwara Sri Tarn Taran Sahib is located at the southeast corner of its sarovar. The sarovar is believed to have healing qualities.

Gurdwara Damdama Sahib

BUILT: 1783
LOCATION: Delhi, India
DESIGN: Sardar Baghel Singh
DESCRIPTION: The Gurdwara Damdama Sahib was built to commemorate a meeting between Guru Gobind Singh and a prince to discuss an upcoming battle. When it was first built, the gurdwara was a small building. Today, it is the center of a large complex that includes a number of religious and administrative buildings. The entire complex is made from white marble. The temple's langar is found on the ground floor. The prayer hall is found on the floor above. The exterior of each floor has a series of domes and towers. The main dome sits on top of a two-story platform.

The Gurdwara Damdama Sahib is known as the place where the writing of the Guru Granth Sahib was completed.

Issues Facing the Sri Harmandir Sahib

The Sri Harmandir Sahib was built hundreds of years ago, when the world was less advanced. Today, more people can visit the shrine than ever before. However, the increased population in and around the structure has put it at greater risk of damage.

WHAT IS THE ISSUE?

The air quality around the Sri Harmandir Sahib is poor due to pollution. This pollution mostly comes from vehicles.

The artwork on the interior has degraded over time.

EFFECTS

Pollution can damage the structure, discoloring the exterior gold and marble.

Paint has chipped and faded. Gold plating has turned black and is coming away from the walls in some places.

ACTION TAKEN

Proposals have been made to limit traffic in the old city of Amritsar near the Sri Harmandir Sahib.

A restoration of the interior was completed in 2014. Damaged artwork was repaired using original materials and techniques.

Water Filtration Activity

Clean water is important not only to the Sri Harmandir Sahib, but to people all over the world. Filtration systems help make sure we have clean water to drink. This experiment shows how water filters remove unwanted material from drinking water.

Materials
- 2-liter plastic soda bottle
- safety scissors
- napkins
- paper towels
- sand
- potting soil
- pebbles
- water
- water pitcher

Instructions

1. With an adult's help, cut the soda bottle in half. Then, put the top half of the bottle into the bottom half, upside down. This will create a funnel through which you can pour the unfiltered water.

2. Place the napkins and paper towels into the soda bottle funnel. These will act as your filter, so pay attention to how you layer these in your funnel. Some of the paper towels and napkins will be thicker and stronger than others.

3. Pour water into the pitcher. Dirty the water by adding sand, potting soil, and pebbles.

4. Pour the dirty water through the filter into the bottle.

5. After the water is poured, pull the filter out of the funnel and examine it. Which layers caught the most dirt? Why do you think these layers worked best?

Sri Harmandir Sahib Quiz

Q Which religious group built the Sri Harmandir Sahib?

A Sikhs

Q How much gold was used to cover the shrine?

A 220 pounds (99.7 kg)

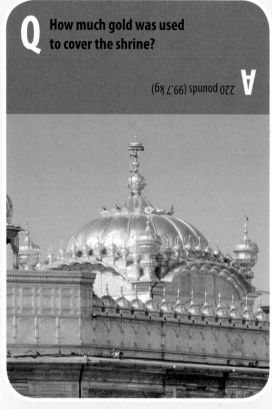

Q What is the pool of water that surrounds the Sri Harmandir Sahib called?

A Sarovar

Q How many entrances does the Sri Harmandir Sahib have?

A Four

Key Words

aqueduct: a channel designed to transport water from a remote source

artisans: craftspeople

causeway: a raised road or path across low or wet ground

clad: to cover material on a building with a protective layer made from another material

excavation: the process of digging a large hole in the ground

filtration: the process of passing a liquid or gas through a device to remove solid particles

foundation stone: a stone laid in a ceremony to celebrate the beginning of construction

gold plate: a thin layer of gold

guru: a spiritual leader or teacher

holy scripture: the sacred writings of a religion

inlaid: set into a surface as decoration

martyr: a person who is killed for his or her beliefs

masonry: stonework

meditation: the practice of focusing concentration in order to reach a higher level of spiritual awareness

militants: people who favor combat as a way of achieving political goals

Muslim: a follower of the faith of Islam

parapet: a low protective wall along the edge of a roof, bridge, or balcony

pinnacle: a tower on the roof of a building

restoration: the return of something to its original condition

seats: centers of authority

shrine: a place regarded as holy

stucco: fine plaster used for coating walls

substructure: the underlying or supporting structure of a building

vaulted: arched to span an opening

Index

Log on to www.av2books.com

AV² by Weigl brings you media enhanced books that support active learning. Go to www.av2books.com, and enter the special code found on page 2 of this book. You will gain access to enriched and enhanced content that supplements and complements this book. Content includes video, audio, weblinks, quizzes, a slide show, and activities.

AV² Online Navigation

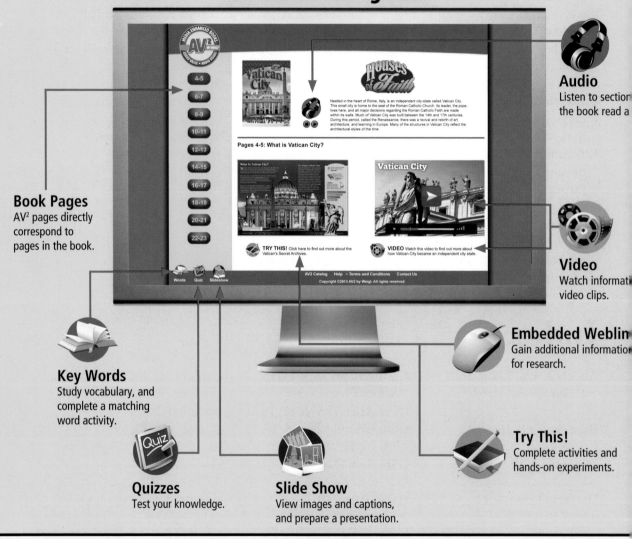

Book Pages
AV² pages directly correspond to pages in the book.

Audio
Listen to section the book read a

Video
Watch informati video clips.

Embedded Weblin
Gain additional informatio for research.

Key Words
Study vocabulary, and complete a matching word activity.

Quizzes
Test your knowledge.

Slide Show
View images and captions, and prepare a presentation.

Try This!
Complete activities and hands-on experiments.

AV² was built to bridge the gap between print and digital. We encourage you to tell us what you like and what you want to see in the future.

Sign up to be an AV² Ambassador at www.av2books.com/ambassador.